LITERATURE & WRITING WORKSHOP

EXPLORING
AUTOBIOGRAPHY

SCHOLASTIC INC.

CONTENTS

BREAKTHROUGH TO THE BIG LEAGUE

by
Jackie Robinson

Illustrated by
Cornelius Van Wright

Less than a week after I joined the Brooklyn club, I played in my first game against the Braves. We won 5-3, but I didn't cover myself with glory. In fact I didn't do well at all that day. I was in another one of those horrible slumps. Playing first base, I grounded to the third baseman in the first inning, flied out to left field, hit into a double play, was safe on error, and later in the game was removed as a defensive safeguard.

I did get one hit.

I am certain the sellout crowd at Ebbets Field was disappointed. I know I was.

I imagine there were some curiosity seekers at that game who had come anticipating trouble because of my presence. They were disappointed. My fellow Dodgers were neither friendly nor hostile. And the Boston boys took everything in stride.

Branch Rickey had been looking around for someone

to replace the benched Leo Durocher. He selected Burt Shotten, who came out of retirement to take over the club.

In that season—1947—it was generally believed that it was Brooklyn's year for the pennant. We had a pretty terrific team. As pitchers there were Ralph Branca, Hank Behrman, Vic Lombardi, Rex Barney, Harry Taylor, Joe Hatten, and in the bullpen, Hugh Casey.

Bruce Edwards was catching; Dixie Walker, Pete Reiser, and Gene Hermanski rotated with Carl Furillo in the outfield. Johnny Jorgensen and Cookie Lavagetto held down third base. Pee Wee Reese was shortstop, Ed Stanky at second, and yours truly on first. In the batting order I was second behind Stanky, the lead-off man.

Manager Shotten and I got along very well, hitting it off right from the beginning.

But not all the news was good.

Ironically, the first big ordeal I was put through in the majors wasn't the work of a deep South team.

The Philadelphia Phillies were the first to create ugliness in my major league career.

We had met our old rivals, the Giants, at the Polo Grounds and given them a 10-4 drubbing. We were in pretty good shape psychologically when the Phillies came to Ebbets Field.

I went to bat in the first inning. As I started toward home plate, members of Ben Chapman's team (our visitors) began shouting insults:

"Go back to the bushes, black boy."

"Hey, nigger. Go back where you came from."

"They're waiting for you in the jungles. We don't want you here, black boy."

I churned up inside but I was prepared. This was the kind of thing Mr. Rickey had foreseen. I wasn't going to let them get the best of me.

The little compliments increased in volume and in profanity as the game went on. I began to notice that my teammates, who up until now had been so noncommittal, were starting to get angry at the Philly bullies.

Ed Stanky, our second baseman, called time and ran over to me.

"Jack," he said, "play this fellow a little closer to the bag."

I believe it was the first time Stanky had given me advice.

"Thanks," I told Ed.

"By the way," he said, patting me on the back, "don't let those bums get you down."

I felt much better prepared for whatever I must take.

The first seven innings were scoreless. We got the Phillies out in the eighth and our team came to bat.

I led off. The insults came from the Phillies' dugout once more.

I let the first pitch go by for a ball and slammed the next one into center field for a single.

The Phillies' pitcher, being a knuckle ball expert, gave me no advantage and I stole second early. Gene Hermanski came up to hit and I took my lead off first. As the Phillies' pitcher let fly, I lit out for second base. On the throw it was wide and bounced past the shortstop as I moved into third. Hermanski singled me home and that decided the ball game.

I felt that the name callers had been answered. Another

answer came from the press. Columnists and editorial writers severely lashed Chapman. In self-defense, the Phillies manager hurriedly called a press conference to explain that, although the name-calling had taken place, his men were not anti-Negro. It seemed they had hurled all this filth at me for the good of my soul. Such treatment, Chapman explained, would make me grow to major league stature. That was the way the Phillies played ball, Chapman said. They had called DiMaggio "the Wop" and Whitey Kurowski "the Polack."

Many people viewed this explanation as a clumsy cover-up. Baseball Commissioner Happy Chandler warned the Phillies to change their habits.

There was one person who wasn't angry with Chapman. Branch Rickey, who usually could see far beyond the obvious, commented happily: "Chapman did more than anybody to make Dixie Walker, Eddie Stanky, and other Dodgers speak up in Robinson's behalf. When he poured out that stream of abuse, he solidified and unified thirty men, not one of whom was willing to sit by and see someone kick a man around who had his hands tied behind his back. Chapman created in Robinson's behalf a thing called sympathy—the most unifying word in the world. That word has a Greek origin; it means to suffer. Thus, to say 'I sympathize with you' means 'I suffer with you.' That is what Chapman did. He caused men like Stanky to suffer with Robinson and he made this Negro a real member of the Dodgers."

As a result of the Chapman incident, I had to submit myself to one of the toughest ordeals I ever faced. I agreed to pose for a picture with Chapman to make the fans feel that we had patched up our differences. My heart wasn't in it. In addition to my lack of respect for Chapman as a man, I learned that when he was asked to pose with me, he agreed on condition that he wouldn't have to shake hands with me and could pose with both of us standing together holding a baseball bat. The only reason I went along with this piece of hypocrisy was that Mr. Rickey sincerely believed it would help the game and the position of the Negro in baseball.

As you can well imagine, things like the Chapman incident were especially hard to take. I don't believe I would have been able to make it in such a tense situation if it hadn't been for the help and guidance I received from two people. These two individuals helped me to maintain control and to concentrate on the positive effort to win friends. From them I learned to avoid being constantly on the defensive, to reject the conclusion that everyone was a potential enemy.

The two people, of course, were Branch Rickey and my wife, Rae. Mr. Rickey's voice and his words were constantly with me. His admonition to "turn the other cheek" came back to me at crucial moments. As for Rae, she was just superb from the beginning. I can remember so often coming home, after a bad day back in Montreal, when I had run into some kind of difficulty. There were times when I believed I was on the verge of a nervous breakdown. I remember the comforting words Rae would say and the way she kissed me. It was that sensitive instinct she had, knowing exactly the right thing to say or do at crucial times, that helped me come back out of any depression.

Much of the strength I got came from my own Dodger teammates. Some of them helped without saying a word—merely by the way they accepted me as a member of the team. Others went so far as to reassure me that they accepted me. There is one ex-teammate of mine whom I will never forget because he was one of the pioneers in speaking up for me when I couldn't speak up for myself.

I am talking about Pee Wee Reese, the talented Brooklyn shortstop. ...

Pee Wee's background made it perfectly natural for him to oppose integrated baseball. He was from Louisville, Kentucky, the same city that gave me such a hard time when I was with Montreal playing against Louisville in the Little World Series. Pee Wee told me his family had expressed some concern about his playing with me. Yet from the very beginning he took a positive attitude about my coming to the Dodgers. ...

"I never met Jackie Robinson," Reese told reporters, (before I actually played with the team), "but I believe he deserves a chance just like anyone else. I've thought about it a great deal and I've tried to put myself in his place. I said to myself: 'Suppose Negroes were in the majority in this country and for years they had barred white players. Then, suppose someone gave me a chance to be the first white player on a Negro team. I'd be so lonely and scared and I sure would appreciate a guy who didn't go out of his way to kick me in the teeth.' So, when I put myself in Robinson's place, I made up my mind that I wasn't going to be the one to give him any kicks in the teeth."

About my possibly taking his job, Pee Wee's answer

was: "There may be enough room in baseball for both of us."

I'll always be grateful that not only was there enough room in baseball for both Pee Wee Reese and Jackie Robinson, but also that he was my teammate and partner on the field. I can tell you that Reese's friendship, his courage in expressing it, and his ability to sense my burdens really fortified me.

I needed that kind of help. Mr. Rickey had been accurate in his predictions of unpleasantness. There was name-calling by fans and by other players. There were snubs and insults. There were viciously pitched balls, aimed at my head. In the early days of my career I won the doubtful distinction of being hit by more of those than any other batter in the league.

There were letters containing threats to hurt my wife, to kill me, to do harm to our baby son, little Jackie, Jr. Crank letters, the police called them. But how was one to know? There were official statements from the Ku Klux Klan, hinting what would happen to me if I came to a certain Dixie town to play ball.

All this was the public part of the abuse which Mr. Rickey had known I would have to face.

There was also a private part.

How cruelly stupid, it seemed, to be living at the center of a group of guys, fighting with them every step of the way during the ball game, and then, when the game was over and you were back in the locker rooms, to find yourself off in your little corner while the rest of the fellows joked and exulted over a victory or tried to mend each other's morale after a defeat. In the early days, after the game was over you didn't see your teammates until it was time to go back to work. They lived in their world and you lived in yours. They lived in the best hotels in town and you lived, maybe, with a private family. Their wives knew each other and were friends. You and your wife got an invitation once in a while to someone's home for dinner or went to a Negro movie house. On trains you sat by yourself or with a Negro newspaperman who might be along. On trains the others played cards and you watched or pretended to be reading a book or a newspaper.

There were times when I felt deeply sorry for myself about these conditions, times when I was humiliated for my wife and child, times when I wondered if the cost of being the first Negro in the majors was going to be worth the reward. There were times when I couldn't sleep or felt so nauseated that I couldn't eat. I was often physically and mentally whipped and worst of all, although I tried to prevent it, sometimes the punishment I was taking was reflected in my performance on the field. ...

I often think back to the times I watched my teammates playing cards and wished I could be part of the game. But one day one of the fellows simply invited me to sit down and join in.

There was one occasion when an ugly incident could have occurred. We were playing cards on the train. Hugh Casey, the Southern-born relief pitcher, startled everyone by declaring: "Tell you what I used to do down in Georgia when my poker luck got bad. I'd just get up and go out and I'd rub me the biggest, blackest nigger woman I could find." He reached over and rubbed my head.

For a second I sat in the tense silence. "Mr. Rickey," I was saying to myself, "I'm sorry, Mr. Rickey. But here goes the *real* Jackie Robinson. No red-blooded Negro lets a white man insult him like this."

The next second I heard the echo of that rumbling voice in Brooklyn.

"I'm looking for a ballplayer, Jackie, with guts enough *not* to fight back." In a blinding flash that cut through my rising anger, I saw that if I lost my temper there would be headlines which would give aid and comfort to everyone who had opposed integration in baseball and cause humiliation to all those who had fought for it.

Quietly I told the man holding the cards to deal.

The tension broke. The game continued. A few days later my teammates had to hold Hugh Casey back because he wanted to rush out on the field to crucify a St. Louis Cardinal player who had spiked me.

Just to keep the record straight, I didn't feel vindicated for having taken Casey's insult just because Casey gave me this approval afterward. No, there was something much more important at stake than Casey's approval. I was an exhibit in a glass cage—a tiger who had been trained not to roar. The day would come when I could roar as loudly as I wished and whenever I pleased. Maybe during these days when I couldn't fight back I could help to fix it so there would be less to roar about in days to come.

Coming back to Pee Wee Reese: Reese not only did things to help ease my private situation; he proved more than once his willingness to put it on the line for me in public. The incident I remember best happened in Boston. By that time Reese and I had become a much talked about double-play combination. In Boston we went out to take our infield practice for the first time in that city. Some of the Boston players began to kid Pee Wee. There wasn't anything vicious about their quips—not as vicious as some of the remarks and insults which had been made by players in other cities. The Boston fellows were kidding Reese, riding him about being from Louisville and playing ball with a Negro. They shouted derisive questions about what this white boy from Louisville and his colored buddy were going to do after the game.

After a few minutes of this, Pee Wee, who hadn't answered a word, left his position and walked over to mine. He didn't even look at the leering Boston team. He placed his hand on my shoulder and began talking to me. I don't think either one of us knew at that time or remembered later what we talked about. What Pee Wee was saying to the Boston boys by his simple gesture was this:

"Yell! Do anything you please. We came here to play baseball. As long as Jackie Robinson does all he possibly can as a ball player to help the Brooklyn club win games, that is all we are asking."

From that minute on there wasn't any more kidding about Pee Wee and me. There were, however, many attempts to drive a wedge between us.

In spite of them, we became close friends—two guys who could talk frankly about how silly it was for anyone to hate anyone else for his color. Pee Wee even asked me to meet the members of his family who had been opposed to our friendship.

By placing the emphasis on what Reese did to help bring

about good will among the Dodgers, I do not mean to slight others on the Brooklyn club who became convinced that they, too, had a contribution to make. Reese was just one of the first and the most constant. I can't forget Ed Stanky, our second baseman when I became a Dodger. From the beginning he was giving me tips about various opposing players, encouraging me, and exhibiting genuine friendship. And Clyde Sukeforth, the scout who had brought me in, also proved most helpful. He did all he could to see me through.

Yet to me, Reese and Branch Rickey symbolize the answer to the differences and the hatreds between people. Mr. Rickey and Reese were the leaders in making a great experiment work. Mr. Rickey had the courage to put me up front. Reese had the daring and the integrity to back me up, leading the way to goodwill between me and my fellow players. I mentioned Ed Stanky before. I remember once, during a particularly nasty exhibition on the part of the opposing team, I was being shouted at and insulted and called every conceivable name.

I didn't reply. Ed Stanky did.

"You yellow-bellied cowards!" Stanky shouted. "Why don't you yell at someone who can answer back?"

Stanky had asked a question which heralded the crack of dawn Branch Rickey had envisioned when he predicted: "The day when your teammates take up the fight for you, that is the day we will have begun to win the battle of integration in baseball."

Back in May of 1947—my first year with the Brooklyn club—we found out how desperate people can become when they are eaten up with hate. A threat which did not involve our personal safety, but which could have wrecked my career, became news that May.

Stanley Woodward of The New York *Herald Tribune* scooped the country by exposing a protest strike planned by members of the St. Louis Cardinals. The plot was that when our team went to play there, they would refuse to play because I was a Dodger. The article stated that some of the Cardinals were attempting to spread such tactics throughout the league to try to keep Negroes out of the game.

Ford Frick, president of the National League, stepped on that one—and fast. Woodward wrote that Frick had informed the players involved that they would be suspended from the league if any such plan materialized.

"You will find that the friends you think you have in the press box will not support you, that you will be outcasts," Frick threatened. "I do not care if half the league strikes. Those who do it will encounter quick retribution. They will be suspended, and I don't care if it wrecks the National League for five years. This is the United States of America, and one citizen has as much right to play as another."

"The National League will go down the line with Robinson whatever the consequence. You will find if you go through with your intention that you have been guilty of complete madness."

That was that.

But if St. Louis had been tamed, there was to be more heard from Philadelphia.

We were beginning a series of games with the Phillies in Shibe Park. During the first game the Phillies again began their name-calling tactics—only with more vehemence this time. They had help from some of the local fans who decided to get into the act.

The second incident with the Phillies brought another official warning from Frick.

"I don't expect Philadelphia or any other team to handle Jackie Robinson with kid gloves," Frick told Philly Manager Chapman, "but let's keep the blows above the belt."

I'll never know to what extent the weight of all these pressures affected my game. I do know that I was in a horrible batting slump. Early in the season, out of twenty-one times at bat, I only got one hit. I was frightened by my failure to produce. I heard rumors that I was going to be benched. Luckily for me, however, both Branch Rickey and Burt Shotten had faith that I would come through.

My old "friends," the Phillies, returned to our home field. There was something about these fellows that really inspired. I felt some of the old power returning, and in the third game of the series I broke through.

In the fourth inning the Phillies were leading 2-0. Leading off, I singled to left field. Four straight hits followed, producing three runs.

Both teams scored later, and in the eighth I had a homer, giving us the insurance run that we needed to move us into third place. We didn't look back from there until we had won the pennant.

I had begun to gain a new confidence. When I joined Montreal, in the beginning of it all, I had a reputation for stealing bases. But with the Dodgers I had held myself down to orthodox patterns. In a night game in Pittsburgh, near the end of June, with the score tied at 2-2, I watched Pitcher Fritz Ostermuller closely. From where I fidgeted at third he appeared to me to be getting a little too relaxed. Something told me to break loose. I danced off third cautiously. Ostermuller wound up, paying me no attention. The pitch was a ball. I eased open my lead off third. When Ostermuller began his windup, I tore out for home plate and slid in safe, loving the roars from the stands.

The stolen run put us out front, 3-2. Some of the Dodgers, excited and happy, came to meet me with congratulations as I ran to the bench. ...

... Some people never want to give up. I've told how the Phillies kept trying to "get" me. The St. Louis Cardinals had their own special brand of persistence. They hadn't been able to get away with the planned strike, but some, though not all, of the players were determined to do something to make things unpleasant.

The St. Louis club came to Brooklyn for a series with us. In the eleventh, Enos Slaughter, the Cardinals' outfielder, spiked me rather cruelly. Fortunately the injury did not prove serious.

The indignation of my fellow Dodgers over the spiking was very deep, and I honestly believe that this feeling was one of the factors which helped bring all of us closer together, united in a fierce determination to answer this kind of sportsmanship with a triumph for our team that season.

I was grateful for the fellowship which began to develop among my fellow players and me.

One thing that had made things tough for me at the beginning was that I had a chip on my shoulder when I first came into the game.

I allowed the newspapers to make me pre-judge the fellows I would be playing with. Back there in 1945 and 1946, the press was saying that the Brooklyn players would not tolerate my presence on the team. There were reams of copy written—some guesses, some derived from actual interview—to the effect that the Dodger members just couldn't bring themselves to be part of interracial baseball. When I first came up on the team, I stayed in my own little corner. I was afraid to try to associate with my teammates. I imagined that there would be riots and fights and that the fellows on the team would do all kinds of vicious things. It didn't take me long to realize that I was wrong. If we were to be successful, I had, in some way, to get along with the fellows in the ball club, to get them to know and understand me. I couldn't expect them to take the giant step all by themselves to create a friendship with me. I had to walk some of the way, too.

With our stronger team spirit we managed to get even with Enos Slaughter and the Cardinals for the spiking I had suffered.

In the next three games we played with them in the series, I got a home run, a double, and four singles in thirteen times at bat—a .462 average. We won two of the three.

At the end of my first season as a Dodger I had played in 151 games, scored 125 runs, hit safely 175 times, batted .297, hit 12 home runs, and led the team in stolen bases.

The *Sporting News,* which had been so negative about the chances of a Negro making good in major league baseball, named me "Rookie of the Year."

I was proud of this, of course, but I was even prouder

that a fight had been won—a fight with myself for self-control. And a firm step forward had been taken not only to bring the Negro into big-league baseball, but also to bring the kind of democracy to the sport which fair-minded people believed America's pastime should have.

There was still a long way to go—for me personally, and for those die-hards who were still opposing the idea. There were so many other people who deserved credit, people like the Wendell Smiths and Billy Rowes who were on the firing line as newspapermen right at the very beginning; people like the Negro ministers and white sociologists and committee folk who kept knocking at the door until it opened just enough to let the first man through; people like Ford Frick and Clay Hopper and players like Stanky and Reese. And Branch Rickey, of course, and Rae Robinson.

But the fight wasn't over.

THE INVISIBLE THREAD

by
Yoshiko Uchida

Illustrated by
Justin Novak

Tub Under The Stars

P apa was a terrible driver. He had taught himself how to drive, and nobody had ever told him to look in both directions before driving through an intersection. Usually he looked one way, and if nothing was coming, he sailed right through with his usual buoyant confidence.

One Sunday afternoon, after we'd taken a friend of Mama's for a drive, Papa made that mistake once too often. Just two blocks from home, Papa came to a corner, looked to the left, and kept going. Unfortunately, another car was coming from the right. And that's when it happened.

We were hit broadside, and our bulky Buick simply toppled over and lay on its side like a beached whale.

Drowsing in the backseat, I was suddenly jolted on top of Mama and proceeded to scream at the top of my lungs. Papa somehow managed to get through the window and pulled the rest of us out.

"Are you all right?" he asked each of us.

"Yes, Papa," we answered feebly. We emerged one by one, to the astonishment of the onlookers who, having heard my screams, probably expected me at least to have a broken arm or leg.

Fortunately, we suffered only minor bumps, cuts, and bruises, and although a bit wobbly, we were able to walk home.

For me the accident was a major event worthy of an illustrated page in my diary, but Papa brushed it aside as a minor inconvenience and kept right on driving as he always had.

One summer he drove us to Livingston to visit Mr. and Mrs. Okubo. They were among the early Japanese Christian families who had settled there, tamed the dry windblown earth, and coaxed grapes to flourish where nothing had grown before. I could hardly wait to spend a few days on a real farm, for I was a child of the city who walked on sidewalks and knew only dogs and cats.

Mama was always nervous about Papa's driving, but after the accident, she was even more so. She usually sat in the back with me, often reaching out to grab my arm whenever Papa went too fast or got too close to a streetcar.

"Be careful, Papa San," she would call out. "You're going too fast." But I don't think Papa ever listened.

Keiko usually sat in front with him because she wanted to watch his every move. Already she had a fairly good idea of how to drive and was dying to get behind the wheel. In a weak moment Papa had said that maybe she could when we got out into the countryside.

As we turned off the main highway, it seemed as though

we were driving through a vast ocean of vineyards that spread out on both sides of the dusty road. Before long we could see the Okubo water pump windmill sprouting up among the grapevines.

"There it is!" Keiko shouted. "There's the Okubo farm!" She reminded Papa of his earlier promise and convinced him there was nothing on the deserted road that she could possibly hit. Papa knew he would never hear the end of it if he didn't give her a chance, so he stopped the car.

Keiko was in heaven as Papa let her slide over behind the wheel. But poor Mama was clutching my arm again.

"Careful, Kei Chan," she cautioned. "Be careful."

Keiko started slowly like a tired turtle. But by the time she made the final turn toward the farm, she was feeling confident and picking up a little speed.

"Honk the horn to let them know we're here," Papa said.

At which point Keiko not only honked the horn, but simultaneously crashed into Jick's dog house, knocked it over on its side, and stopped just inches short of the walnut tree.

"Look out, for heaven's sake," we all shouted. "Look out!"

Jick barked furiously at the sudden assault on his territory, and the chickens scrambled in every direction, screeching and cackling as though the end of the world had come.

The startled Okubos rushed from their house, blinking in the sun, surveying with alarm what only moments before had been their peaceful yard.

"We're here!" Keiko shouted, as if they needed to be told. "We're here!"

Because the Okubos' two grown daughters had already

left home, they welcomed my sister and me as though we were their grandchildren, and we called them Oji San (uncle) and Oba San (auntie).

Oji San gave us a quick tour of the farm. He showed us how to pump water from the well and put our heads down to gulp the cold water that came gushing out. He pointed to the outhouse, saying, "I guess you've never used one of those before." We certainly hadn't. Whenever I had to use it, I held my breath and got out as fast as I could.

He also let us look for eggs in the hen house, and took us to the barn where we staggered about in the hayloft, trying to pitch hay with forks that were bigger than we were.

He saved the best for last, taking us to a fenced enclosure where two dusty mules ambled over to greet us.

"Meet Tom and Jerry," he said. Then, pulling some scraggly weeds by the fence, he told us to feed them to the mules.

I thrust some weeds at them and the mules grabbed them hungrily, showing their enormous yellow teeth. They seemed friendly enough, but I was rather glad they were on the other side of the fence.

"They like you." Oji San said. "Maybe they'll do something nice for you later on."

"Like what, Oji San?"

Oji San just grinned and smashed his felt hat down over his forehead. "You'll see," he said. "Wait and see."

Sitting on mats spread out under the walnut tree, we had a wonderful picnic supper of soy-drenched chicken and corn grilled over an outdoor pit. There were rice balls, too, sprinkled with black sesame seeds that looked like tiny ants.

Oji San waited until the sun had dipped down behind the dusty grapevines and a soft dusky haze settled in the air. Then he announced he was taking us all on a moonlight ride through the vineyards. It was more than we'd ever hoped for.

Keiko took her usual place up front by Oji San, hoping for a brief chance at the reins. Mama and Papa chatted quietly with Oba San, and I lay stretched out in back, looking up at the enormous night sky.

There seemed to be millions and billions of stars up there. More than I'd ever imagined existed in the universe. They seemed brighter and closer than they were in Berkeley. It was as though the entire sky had dropped closer to Earth to spread out its full glory right there in front of me.

I listened to the slow clop-clop of the mules as they plodded through the fields, probably wondering why they were pulling a wagonload of people in the dark, instead of hauling boxes of grapes to the shed under the hot, dry sun.

I could hear crickets singing and frogs croaking and all the other gentle night sounds of the country. I felt as though I were in another more immense, never-ending world, and wished I could keep riding forever to the ends of the Earth.

When we got back to the farm, it was time for an outdoor Japanese bath. Oji San built a fire under a square tin tub filled with water, banking the fire when the water was hot and inserting a wooden float so we wouldn't burn our feet or backsides when we got in.

Oba San hung some sheets on ropes strung around the tub and called out, *"Sah, ofuro!* Come, Kei Chan, Yo Chan. The bath is ready. You girls go first."

Mama gave us careful instructions about proper bathing procedures. "Wash and rinse yourselves outside before you get into the tub," she reminded us. "And keep the water clean."

When we were ready to climb in, I saw steam rising from the water and was afraid I'd be boiled alive. "You go first," I told my sister.

As always, Keiko was fearless. She jumped right in and sank down in the steaming water up to her neck.

"Ooooooh, this feels wonderful!" she said.

I quickly squeezed in next to her, and we let the warm water gurgle up to our chins.

Keiko looked up at the glorious night sky and sighed, "I could stay here forever."

"Where? In the tub?"

Foreigner In Japan

I was twelve when we sailed on the *Chichibu Maru* to visit my Grandmother Umegaki in Japan. My parents had taken me once before when I was two, but since I didn't remember that visit, I felt it didn't count. This time we were taking along our Los Angeles grandmother for her first visit to Japan since her departure so many years before.

I considered this my first ocean voyage, although I had gone often with my parents to see friends off at the drafty San Francisco piers. We would be among dozens of well-wishers crowding on board the ship to visit friends in staterooms bursting with luggage, flowers, and baskets of fruit. Caught up in the festive excitement, I used to wish *I* were the one sailing off to Japan.

When one of the cabin boys traveled through the corridors beating the brass gong, however, I always felt a cold chill run down my spine.

"Come on, Papa," I would urge. "That's the 'all ashore that's going ashore' gong. Let's go."

But Papa continued talking with his friends, totally ignoring the urgent banging of the gong. By the time the passengers moved to the deck to throw rolls of colored tape to their friends below, the rest of us hurried down the narrow gangplank.

Papa, however, was still on board, smiling and waving from the upper deck. He would throw a roll of blue tape to my sister and a pink one to me.

"Come on, Papa!" we would shriek. "Hurry up!"

Finally, minutes before the gangplank was pulled up, he would saunter down, calmly saying, "Don't worry, they would never sail with me still on board."

Papa had a permanent dock pass to board the ships, and he came so often to meet friends or to see people off that he seemed to know everybody. For him the ships were familiar territory, but to me they were exotic, majestic, and slightly mysterious.

But this time, at last, I didn't have to worry about Papa getting caught on board a departing ship. This time we were passengers. *We* were the ones sailing to Japan. We were the ones everybody had come to see off. The baskets of fruits and flowers in the stateroom from Papa's business friends were for *us*. So were the gardenia corsages and the bouquets of flowers.

Now *I* was the one throwing rolls of tape down to our friends on the pier and waving and calling good-bye.

As the ship slowly eased out into San Francisco Bay, the wind tugged at the streamers I held in my hand. But I wouldn't let go. I hung on until the ship snatched them from the hands of the friends we'd left behind, and I watched as they fluttered off into the sky looking like a flying rainbow.

"Hey, we're really going!" I said to Keiko. "We're really going to Japan!"

But ten minutes after we had sailed through the Golden Gate, the ship began to pitch and roll, and my happy grin soon disappeared. The ever-present smell of bouillon I'd found so inviting earlier now made me turn green. All of us except Papa took to our bunks and stayed there for the next four days.

When we were finally able to join Papa in the dining salon, our waiters were so pleased to have a full table to serve, they broke into applause as we appeared.

By this time all shipboard activities were in full swing, and Keiko and I worked hard to catch up. We played shuffleboard and deck tennis. We had hot bouillon served by white-coated boys who rolled the soup cart up and down the decks each morning at ten o'clock. We went to every afternoon tea, stuffing ourselves with little cakes and fancy sandwiches, and amazingly had room for a big dinner in the evening

One night there was a sukiyaki party on the lantern-festooned deck. For once I didn't have to set the table and neither Mama nor Papa had to cook. We were the company, and I was delighted that the ship's waiters did all the work. The Deans of Women of Mills College and the University of California in Berkeley happened to sit at our table, and we showed them how to use chopsticks and eat Japanese food.

"You'll have to send one of your daughters to each of us," they teased Mama and Papa. And that is exactly what happened. Keiko went to Mills College and I went to U.C. Berkeley.

The day a costume party was scheduled, Keiko and I worked all day to prepare for it. She wore a pair of Papa's pants and suspenders, drew a mustache on her face, and squashed one of his hats on her head.

I dressed up like a doll, painting round circles of rouge on my cheeks. We tied strings to my wrists and ankles, attached them to two sticks, and went to the costume party as Tony the puppeteer and his doll puppet. We were beside ourselves when we won first prize.

By the time we neared Yokohama, I was so charmed with the good life on board the *Chichibu Maru,* I didn't want to get off.

Mama, on the other hand, could hardly wait. The morning we docked, she was up early. As our ship slid noiselessly alongside the pier, she impulsively pushed open one of the cabin's portholes to scan the faces on the pier.

Suddenly I heard her shout "Oka San! Mother!"

It was a voice I had never heard before—filled with the longing and anguish of years of separation and a joy mingled with tears.

This was a Mama I'd never known before. For the first time in my life, I saw her not just as Mama who cooked and washed and sewed for us, but as someone's daughter. She was a person with a life and feelings of her own quite apart from mine.

For a fleeting moment I thought I understood the turmoil of her uprooted soul. But in the excitement of landing, the feeling passed, and she became once more the Mama I had always known.

None of us ever dreamed then of the terrible war that would separate her from her family and homeland forever.

It was a wonder to me how Mama could have left behind

such a nice family and so many good friends. We met them all while we were in Japan.

Grandmother Umegaki was a plump, friendly woman with a quiet manner that belied her strength. It was that hidden strength that gave her the courage to send her oldest daughter to America, and I believe my mother had a good measure of it in herself as well.

Mama's brother, Yukio, was a silversmith who made all sorts of beautiful gifts for us—a copper hanging engraved with my mother's favorite wildflower, a silver pin of my dog for me, and an engraved silver buckle for Keiko.

Another brother, Minoru, was a college professor who was writing several scholarly books and also painted quite well. I wasn't sure how to behave in front of Seizo, the brother who had become a priest, but he turned out to be the most fun of all, and a skilled artist as well.

All three uncles wrote wonderful illustrated letters to my sister and me until the war ended their correspondence, and the life of one uncle as well.

Mama's only sister, Kiyo, was a widow who had lost a baby son and lived with her only daughter. They both seemed permanently saddened by their losses and had none of the easy laughter that dwelled in Mama and her brothers.

We were surrounded by family in Japan, since two of Papa's sisters had returned to live there as well. One lived in Osaka and the other in Tokyo. Wherever we went, we seemed to have a place to stay. Our relatives simply spread out some quilts for us on the *tatami* mat, enclosed us in great billowing mosquito netting, and we were set for the night.

One of the happiest times for my parents and Grandma Uchida was our stay in Kyoto, with its temples and hills and their beloved Doshisha University. The first friends Oba San wanted to visit were Dr. and Mrs. Learned, for whom she had worked so long ago.

They seemed so old and frail to me, like pale white shadows in a sea of Japanese faces. They showered us with love and affection, and gave Keiko and me the American names we had long wanted to have. Keiko was named Grace, and I was given the name Ruth. But somehow it didn't make me as happy as I thought it would. I just didn't feel like a Ruth, and I never used the name.

Keiko and I tolerated innumerable long dinners and lunches with our parents' many friends, but when things get too boring, we would count the number of times people bowed to each other. In Japan no one hugged or shook hands. They just bowed. And bowed. And bowed some more. My mother set the record, with thirteen bows

exchanged in one encounter.

What I liked best was going to temples and shrines on festival days, when the celebration, with costumed dancers and booming drums, was like a holiday parade and carnival rolled into one.

But I liked the celebration of Obon (All Souls' Day), too. That was when the spirits of the dead were believed to return home, and some families lit tiny bonfires at their front gate to welcome them at dusk. Inside, there were tables laden with all sorts of delicious dishes, prepared especially for the returning spirits.

In Japan the dead seemed to blend in with the living, as though there were no great black separation by death. And I found that a comforting thought.

Sometimes we climbed wooded hills that rose behind ancient temples to visit graveyards filled with moss-covered tombstones. And one day we went to pay our respects to our samurai grandfathers, whom we had never known. Using small wooden scoops, we poured cold water on their tombstones to refresh their spirits, and left them handfuls of summer lilies.

I wondered what they thought of us—their grandchildren from far-off America, dressed in strange clothing and babbling in a foreign tongue. I hoped they liked us.

Once we stayed with an uncle and some cousins at a rural inn, where at the end of the day, we all went to the communal tub to have a pleasant soak together.

Then, wearing cool cotton kimonos provided by the inn, we gathered around the low table, where the maids brought us miso soup, broiled eel, and slivered cucumber on individual black lacquer trays.

After dinner we sat on the verandah and had sweet bean

paste cakes and tea, watching a full moon rise over the mountains. The talk was gentle, and whenever it stopped, we could hear the swarms of cicadas in the pine trees buzzing in unison like some demented chorus.

As I sat watching the fireflies darting about in the darkness, I thought maybe I could get quite used to living in Japan. Here, at least, I looked like everyone else. Here, I blended in and wasn't always the one who was different.

And yet, I knew I was really a foreigner in Japan. I had felt like a complete idiot when an old woman asked me to read a bus sign for her, and I had to admit I couldn't read Japanese.

Deep down inside, where I really dwelled, I was thoroughly American. I missed my own language and the casual banter with friends. I longed for hot dogs and chocolate sodas and bathrooms with plumbing.

But the sad truth was, in America, too, I was perceived as a foreigner.

So what was I anyway, I wondered. I wasn't really totally American, and I wasn't totally Japanese. I was a mixture of the two, and I could never be anything else.

THE MOON AND I

by
Betsy Byars

Illustrated by
Robert Sauber

A Snake Named Moon

I glanced up and saw it.
Snake, I said to myself. That looks like a snake.
I got up out of my porch rocking chair and went closer.

That *is* a snake.

I stopped moving closer.

The snake lay on an overhead beam. It was long and slender. It was doubled back over its body, its head pillowed on one of its loops. The snake was so dark in color, it looked black. The eyes were round, the stare unblinking—and the round, unblinking eyes were looking at me.

I had been sitting on the porch for an hour, editing one of my books, and for an hour this snake had been watching me.

Now I don't like anybody watching me when I'm writing—particularly snakes.

I can't even write when my dog's watching. My dog can

lie down under the word processor and sleep—that's fine, but when he starts watching, I can't write. I have to say, "Want to go for a *walk*?" *Walk* and *sup-per* are my dog's favorite words. I can't keep saying, "Want *sup-per?*" or the dog would end up weighing a thousand pounds.

Here's the way I write a book:

• I start on the word processor and write as much as I can. Then I print it.

• I take what I've printed, go sit somewhere else—like the porch—read it, say, "This is terrible," and start working on it.

• I go back to the word processor, put in the changes, and print it.

• I take what I've printed, go sit somewhere else, say, "Oh, this is *still* terrible," and rewrite it.

• I keep doing this until I say, "This is not as terrible as it used to be," then, "This is getting better," and finally (hopefully), "This is not bad at all."

That's how I do my writing, no matter what kind it is—short stories, essays, novels. And it's worked for thirty years.

So, I was on the porch saying, "This is *still* terrible," when I looked up and saw this snake coiled high on one of the beams.

I moved my rocking chair back a bit. If the snake dropped off the beam, it could land on my lap. Nobody wants a lapful of snake.

I settled down to watch.

The snake continued to lie in its relaxed coil. It shifted position occasionally—stretching out full length, recoiling, curving, but it never moved from the beam.

I didn't know much about snakes, but the color—black—was comforting. Blacksnakes are harmless and beneficial. They go after mice, which I had a few of and which they were welcome to.

This snake was obviously not on the prowl at the moment. It might even be digesting one of my mice. Slowly the snake raised its head, and I saw the startling milky white of the chin and throat. I decided to call my husband for a second opinion.

"Yes" it's a blacksnake," Ed confirmed.

"But the throat is white. Are you sure blacksnakes have white throats?"

"Yes."

"Blacksnakes don't... er... bite, do they?"

"They can."

"Oh."

"But their bite is never more than a scratch."

"Ah."

I was gaining confidence.

"If cornered, the blacksnake will put up a good front," he went on. "It will even shake its tail like a rattler, but it's not a good fighter. Sometimes it becomes so frantic it bites its own body. ''

That was my kind of snake.

There was a pause while my husband and I admired the snake, and the snake allowed us to.

"Have you got a heavy plastic garbage bag?" my husband asked abruptly.

"Garbage bag? What do you want a garbage bag for?" "I think I'll take the snake to the airport," Ed said. His hangar at the airport was troubled by mice.

My reaction was instant and protective. "You can't have it." I said. "It's mine."

Meeting a snake on my front porch had been a pleasant distraction, and I like distractions—especially when I'm writing. After a while, however, I went back inside to the word processor. The window in the room where I work faces out onto the porch, and I got up frequently to check on what was now "my snake."

The snake was always there, but its position changed every time I looked. Sometimes the snake was draped around the beam like a scarf. Sometimes the snake's tail dangled below. Sometimes the head was tucked out of sight, under the body. Whatever the position, it was graceful and pleasing to watch.

As the afternoon wore on, my snake checks became more frequent. I didn't think the snake would spend the night on the porch, and I wanted to see where it went after it left. I wanted to see it slither down the wisteria vine— which was probably how it got up on the porch in the first place—and I wanted to see where it went

Then something happened to me. I became totally engrossed in what I was writing.

Now, most of the time I plod along, writing word by word, sentence by sentence. But then sometimes, suddenly— it's like switching to a higher gear in a car—I take off.

That's what happened now—I took off. I wrote furiously for about an hour. It was as if an invisible dam had burst, and my fingers on the keyboard could barely keep up with my mind.

It was six o'clock when the magical flow stopped. My thoughts immediately returned to the snake, and I jumped up and went to the window.

The snake was gone.

Of all the stupid things to do—I had let my writing get in the way of my snake watching!

Disappearances upset me—a lot.

I felt exactly like I did the time I left my word processor for less than a minute—one minute!—and I discovered when I got back that the chapter I had been working on had disappeared! An entire chapter had vanished!

Later, when I was more rational, I figured up exactly how long I was away from the word processor. Here are my calculations:

Walk to refrigerator	11 seconds
Take miniature Snickers from freezer	3 seconds
Warm Snickers in microwave	16 seconds
Return eating Snickers	11 seconds
Total elapsed time	41 seconds

And in forty-one seconds a whole chapter disappeared! Vanished! To this day I don't know where that chapter went!

And that chapter was perfect! It was the only perfect chapter I have ever done in my life!

And now, instead of a perfect chapter, I had a blank screen! I freaked.

I started pressing keys. I paged up. I paged down. I punched escape (which I had been saving to punch when I was truly desperate). I punched home, end, scroll, control, F1, F2, F3 ... AF1, AF2...

You name it, I punched it.

My last desperate punch was AF10. Then I stored. UNDER WHAT NAME?

BS (BS stood for Blank Space, because subconsciously I knew even then that was what I was storing.)

FILE STORED ON DISK. YOUR CHOICE?

RETRIEVE

WHICH FILE?

BS

I waited with my heart in my throat only to have my worst fears realized. I had indeed stored—and I now retrieved—a blank space.

At that point I did the only sensible thing left to do. I turned off the word processor and went back to the refrigerator for another miniature Snickers.

(Actually, it's no wonder I don't want anybody watching me write.)

Now it was the same thing all over again. I had had a perfect snake. Now I had a blank space. And worst of all, I didn't even have a retrieve key to press.

E!G!G!S!

The first time I owned a snake I was 7 years old, and the snake was mine for about fifteen glorious minutes.

Back then I didn't want to be a writer. I didn't know any writers—I had never even seen one—but their photographs looked funny, as if they'd been taken to a taxidermist and stuffed.

I read a lot, so I saw many dust-jacket photographs, and it seemed to me that no matter how hard authors tried— the men put pipes in their mouths and the women held little dogs—nothing helped. Authors, even my favorites, looked nothing like the kind of person I wanted to become.

This corpselike look, I figured, came from sitting alone all day in a room typing, which couldn't be good for you. Oh sure, I was glad there were people willing to do this. I loved books and didn't want them to become extinct. But I cared too much about myself and my future to consider becoming one of them. When I grew up I was going to work in a zoo. I would take care of the baby animals whose mothers had rejected them. I envisioned myself in an attractive safari outfit feeding lion cubs and other exotic offspring from a bottle.

In preparation for this life my best friend, Wilma, and I

played "Zoo" a lot. This consisted of setting up zoos in the backyard and begging people to come and view the exhibits.

The bug exhibit was always the largest but drew the least attention. Ants, doodlebugs, beetles went unacclaimed—even lightning bugs, since the zoo was not open at night and their daytime "thing" was resting on the underside of leaves.

Tadpoles (in season) were a popular exhibit, especially when the legs started coming out. Slugs had a certain "yuck" appeal, as did leeches (which we got by wading in a forbidden creek and pulling them off our ankles).

Butterflies were popular, but also seasonal, and the favorite exhibits were the snails and box turtles, which, in addition, required little maintenance.

Admission was free.

Wilma and I were always on the alert for new acquisitions and went about regularly during the summer months turning over stones and rotten logs.

One July afternoon Wilma and I set out, followed by my goat Buttsy, who liked to be in on things. While the three of us were rooting through the woodpile, we came across some eggs. The eggs were buried in the rotten sawdust at the bottom of the pile.

And these were not just eggs. These were E!G!G!S! We said the word so many times with so many different inflections that it no longer sounded like a word but more like an inhuman cry of triumph.

The eggs were capsule-shaped, about two inches long, and leathery in appearance. There were about a dozen of them. They weren't hard like hen's eggs but were elastic and tough. They were light in color—an almond white—and smooth.

These were really and truly E!G!G!S!

When we calmed down at last, a disagreement followed over what should be done with them.

There were three possibilities.

Wilma brought up the first. She would take them home with her.

I reminded Wilma of the violent reaction her mother had had to our trained cicadas.

This had happened one day when Wilma and I were training cicadas on her screen porch. This was with an eye to a future circus.

We would start the cicadas up the screen. When they were halfway up, we would tap the screen—sharply—and the cicadas would immediately turn around and go back down. That had been the extent of the training, but we had more complex tricks in mind.

"Get the bugs off the porch," Wilma's mother had said. "Mom, they aren't bugs, they're cicadas." "Get-the-bugs-off- the- porch." "Mom, we're training them."

"Train them over at Betsy's house." "We can't! Betsy doesn't have a screen porch!"

"Now!"

The second possibility—my own—was that I would take the eggs home with me.

Wilma reminded me of the violent reaction my mother had had to the leeches.

This happened the first time we came upon leeches and didn't know what they were. In our enthusiasm we ran up from the creek to show everybody the weird brown things on our ankles that didn't want to come off.

"Leeches!" my sister had cried in a way that let us know weird brown things were not a good thing to have on our ankles. "Mother, Betsy's got leeches on her ankles!"

My mother came out of the house, got a sharp stick and pried my leeches off. This hurt enough to make me cry. When Wilma heard my cries of pain, she quickly got her own sharp stick and pried hers off herself.

"I don't ever want to see you with leeches on your ankles again," my mother said with a shake of the leech stick.

"You won't," I answered, still tearful.

And she never did, because Wilma and I pried the leeches off the minute we got out of the creek, before they had time to stick. The leech display, while not popular with adults, was one of our regulars.

The third, and less appealing possibility, was to leave the eggs where they were.

We compromised.

Wilma put two of the eggs and some sawdust in her mayonnaise jar—the holes were already in the lid. I put two of the eggs and some sawdust in my mayonnaise jar— ditto on the holes—and we left the rest in the woodpile.

The eggs stuck together a little bit, but we managed to get four separated without breaking anything—including our friendship.

"Be careful! Be careful!"

"I am being careful. You're the one who's not being careful." The eggs weren't slimy, but they were moist, and Wilma and I promised to water ours faithfully.

We thought—hoped!—the eggs were snake eggs, but we agreed, like future parents, that we would not be the least disappointed in baby turtles.

Wilma's eggs never got the opportunity to hatch because Wilma's sister said, "Mother, Wilma put some funny-looking eggs in our sock drawer."

Wilma had three sisters and they all wore the same size socks and borrowed from each other, so this was not exactly a clever hiding place.

Wilma's mother promptly flushed her eggs down the toilet. I hid my mayonnaise jar in the back of my closet. I checked my eggs often—like two hundred times a day. About a week after I had put the mayonnaise jar behind my roller skates, one of the eggs looked different. It seemed to move. I took the jar to the window.

A slit appeared in the egg.

Fluid leaked out.

A small snout appeared.

"Everybody! Everybody! My egg is hatching!" The hatching took about a day. The jar was allowed a place of honor in the center of the kitchen table, and we all watched—I with my chin resting on my hands, staring into the glass.

By the time the snake emerged—it took its time—the egg casing had been slashed to ribbons.

The snake was small—about six inches in length—and absolutely perfect. It was brownish. My father said it was a bullsnake.

My father held it in his hand and it crawled and twisted in a lively manner. Then I held it in my hand. It was like holding a strand of electrified brown spaghetti.

I dropped it and it got into a perfect striking position. Its tail shook.

My father said, "When a snake wags its tail at you, it's not being friendly."

After that my mother made me put the snake back in the mayonnaise jar, take it out in the yard, and let it go. "I want to keep it! I have to keep it! I'll take care of it myself! You won't have to do a thing! I'll keep the lid on the jar! I'll feed it and clean the case and—"

"Now."

"Motherrrrrr…"

"Now!"

I released the baby bullsnake in the field beside our house. I watched it slither away into the tall grass with the painful, heartbreaking regret that only a 7-year-old who *needs* a snake can know.

Back then, one of the reasons I wanted to become an adult was so that I could have as many pets as I wanted. My list was long. It started out:

• As many dogs as possible.

• At least two horses—male and female—and all of their colts.

• A goat exactly like my goat Buttsy (who had recently died and whom I missed every time I got in the hammock—Buttsy used to push me).

Now I added to the list:

• Pet snake, preferably nonpoisonous.

So when I saw the snake on my front porch that July afternoon, it was as if a childish dream, long forgotten, had come true at last.

And now the dream was gone!

The Missing Moon

I rushed out onto the porch. The first thing I checked was the wisteria vine. The twisting tentacles look enough like a snake to be one—no snake.

I checked the maple tree. The limbs touch the porch in a few places. A snake could possibly… if it knew exactly which limb to reach for… no snake.

I sat down in a rocker and sighed with disappointment. And this snake had been perfect! It was the first perfect snake I had seen in fifty years and now it was gone!

Vanished! This was worse than losing a chapter.

And, let's face it, a chapter can be rewritten. Maybe it won't be perfect, but it will be a chapter. Anyway, a chapter that was absolutely perfect might make the rest of the chapters look bad.

But with a snake...

I heard a noise.

I got up and glanced over the porch railing. There was the snake on the ground, covered in an angle of the chimney. A neighbor's calico cat—Ginger—held it in place.

My heart actually leapt, like in poetry.

Thank you, Ginger.

Ginger and the snake were involved in a tense, eyeball-to-eyeball face-off.

The sounds I had heard were coming from the cat. These were low, throaty growls that couldn't have had much effect, because snakes don't have ears.

The snake remained coiled, silent, alert, and ready. The tip of its tail began to quiver.

Perhaps, I thought, the snake was gearing up for one of those brave, absurd fights my husband had spoken of. I was torn between wanting to see the snake in action and not wanting to see it bite its own body.

Like a mother whose child is threatened, I slapped my hands against the side of the railing.

"Go home, Ginger!"

The cat looked up, startled. Then she dashed into the woods, taking the shortcut for home.

My snake remained for a moment, testing the climate with flicks of its dark, forked tongue. Then, apparently satisfied that the danger had passed, the snake began uncoiling. The black color was startling against the green ivy, and I could see that the snake was longer than I had thought—about six feet.

The snake began to move in a series of graceful S-curves, its head a few inches off the ground.

It circled the chimney. The movement was as slick as mercury.

The chimney began to block the snake's path from my view, and I wanted to see where it was going. I did not want another disappearance.

I rushed into the living room, dashed around the sofa, and threw open the sliding door to the back deck.

I went out and leaned over the railing, waiting... waiting... The snake did not appear.

After a moment I accepted the fact that the snake was not going to appear. I walked down the steps, paused to check the path, and then walked slowly down the path. I was looking for a hole or a crevice where the snake could have disappeared.

No hole, no crevice... no snake.

Suspecting that the snake had been fast enough to get under the deck before I—with all my speed—could get to the deck, I knelt and peered through the dusty, late-afternoon sunlight.

No snake.

With a sigh I went back inside the house to turn off the word processor.

At the end of a writing day the last thing I do is take the pages I have completed, punch three holes in them, and fit them into a loose-leaf notebook.

I take this notebook home with me. I write at my log house, but I live about five minutes away in a condominium on Lake Hartwell. Sometimes I even get a flash of inspiration on the way home and pull over onto the side of the road to scribble.

This night I did no scribbling. My notebook remained closed. Snakes are much, much more interesting than manuscripts.

"Guess what?" I said to my grandson over the phone that night.

"What?"

"I have a pet snake!"

"Where did you get it?"

"It came up on my porch."

"Does it have a name?"

"Moon," I said, without missing a beat

"Granny, Moon's not a good name for a snake."

"Yes, it is, because the first time I saw this snake, it was high over my head. And ever since then it's brought a nice glow to my life."

"Then Moon is a good name for a snake."

"And," I went on, "the reason I call it my 'pet' snake is not because I keep it in a case or anything. The word pet means favorite. So this is my favorite snake. That's why I say it's my pet snake."

"I wish I had a pet snake.

"They are nice."

"I hope I'll get to see Moon sometime."

"I hope you will, too."

End of pet snake discussion.

And probably, I thought regretfully as I hung up the phone, end of Moon.

"Everyone is a moon," Mark Twain said, "and has a dark side which he never shows to anybody."

I didn't think of Mark Twain's quotation when I gave Moon that name, but it wouldn't be long before I would see its dark side.

Only A Cardboard Moon

The main characters of this book will be:

1. A snake named Moon

2. A writer named Betsy Byars

The time and setting will be:

1. A log house (today)

2. A rural neighborhood in Charlotte, N.C. (fifty years ago)

The plots will be:

1. The writer, Betsy Byars, comes to know a snake, Moon, and blah... blah... blah.

That is not the way I start a book. Here is the way I start a book:

THE MOON AND I

by

Betsy Byars

This book was set in Cheltenham

and composed by Marjorie Campolongo.

It was printed on 50 lb. Finch Opaque.

Title page illustration by Ken Joudrey

Editor: Deborah Jerome-Cohen

Design: Patricia Isaza